Don't Go to College, Go to Europe for Less

Jimmy Huston

International Edition

Cosworth Publishing
21545 Yucatan Avenue
Woodland Hills CA 91364
www.cosworthpublishing.com

For information regarding permission,
please send an email to *office@cosworthpublishing.com*.

This book is dedicated to paying off student loans.

Table of Contents

Top Ten Reasons Not to Go to College

1. Too damned expensive.

2. Costs too much.

3. Ridiculously out of reach financially.

4. You can't afford it.

5. You don't have enough money.

6. It's really just for rich folks.

7. Priced out of reach.

8. Not worth the money.

9. Overslept.

10. Too damned expensive.

Introduction

This is a silly book.

You already know the general premise and you know it's ridiculous – but you're reading anyway. That's good. It may mean that you have an open mind (which college would probably slam shut).

This book isn't for everyone. If you're going to be a surgeon, by all means go to college. Or an astronaut. You'll go to Europe later, when you're in your fifties. Sure, you'll be looking at all the kids around you having fun and wishing you'd done it earlier, but you'll know you made the practical decision instead. Good for you.

Granted, there are many fields where resumes are critical and studies are essential, so perhaps college is for you. Good luck, and please hand this book to another kid (or parent).

If, however, you're having doubts, this book provides an arguably acceptable alternative.

It would be spurious to suggest that Bill Gates, Mark Zuckerberg, and Steve Jobs were college dropouts, except that – well, they were. Admittedly, their situation is not remotely the same as yours but things worked out pretty well for them as they transformed modern life around the entire globe and became incredibly wealthy. But – their parents wanted them to go to college.

There is no rational conventional explanation for these dropouts' behavior, going against the grain in every sense. They'll be sorry. No reunion.

Most readers of this book are probably high schoolers who are approaching graduation. Maybe you've looked around and noticed that you can't get a very good job with just a high school diploma. To most bosses you're still a kid and you don't know much about anything. They're not about to give you a high paying job, or even a decent paying job. You're too damn young. So maybe you should hide out in college for four years.

That's the grownups' dirty little secret – that college is just to keep you off the streets until you're old enough to get a decent job. Sure, you'll learn something in college, but you'd also learn stuff if you spent four years in prison or just about anywhere else except for a coma.

You've already been in school for twelve or more

years and that didn't do it. Why is another four years going to suddenly do the trick? Maybe there's another way.

There's Europe.

This is *not* a vacation. To be successful you will have to put every bit as much work and thought into this venture as you would four years of college. As a result, you will inadvertently become educated.

No tests. No grades. No student debt.

This is a serious book.

Chapter One

Skip College? Really?

After high school, Federico Fellini enrolled in law school, but never attended a single class. A college dropout – doomed – he barely won five Oscars, the Legion of Honor, and the Praemium Imperiale, considered to be on the level of the Nobel Prize.

Admittedly, this book presents a dangerous idea. In order for it to work, you'll have to be ambitious, aggressive, relentless, and personable. You're going to have to rethink everything you know about how things work – but then that's the whole idea anyway.

Instead of spending four years in some stupid dorm room living with a stranger chosen at random

– spend that time traveling in Europe.

You're not going to be a tourist – a visitor. You're going to be a *resident.* An urban guerrilla.

You probably have doubts about college already. Maybe it's been "the plan" for as long as you can remember. Maybe your parents expect it. Or demand it.

But –

College is static. Even the best college is essentially a bunch of buildings with lots of people scrambling around inside them, trying to gain an edge. In any college you're going to spend a lot of time sitting in a room listening to someone tell you things that you won't remember. Sure, there'll be activities and projects and discussions, but it's mostly a crock.

There's always the chance that you'll meet a wise man or woman who will mentor you and change your life. But ask around. It happens, but not for everyone. Not for most people. Most of your teachers and professors are only concerned about getting published, or applying for a grant, or reaching tenure. The rest of your instructors will be graduate students who are only a few pages ahead of you in the textbook.

In olden days, young men would leave home and travel to places of distinction to learn the ways of the world and seek their fortunes. Even the young women of renowned had to strike out on their own, though it wasn't usually approved of.

So, besides your parents, who's been telling you that you need a college degree?

Teachers!

What does college do? It provides jobs for teachers! And it creates too many college graduates who aren't qualified to do anything except teach, thus extending the cycle. By the way, ask your teachers if they've been to Europe. Many can't afford it because they're paying off student loans.

College is not the only path and there are certainly young people who are not college bound. Plenty of good, honorable jobs require training, but not college. There are factory jobs, service jobs, construction jobs, and such – mostly good-paying blue collar jobs – and some even offer the possibility of advancement into careers in management. It's worth mentioning that many of these jobs require physical labor and some of them require workers to get dirty. There's nothing wrong with that, but it's a choice

you have to live with, perhaps for a long, long time.

Traditional apprenticeships have been around for centuries, preparing young people for jobs. These paths were rigid and tedious, never leading beyond the trade they supported, but they worked.

Today, some non-college kids choose to enlist in the armed forces, partly because of the siren call to "See the World!" The assumption is that their time in the service will provide a broad spectrum of experience, training and, in many cases, travel to exotic lands. That sounds like a good idea.

The hidden flaw in this course of action is that there is a tacit, unspoken understanding that your primary obligation is to support an unspecified potential war effort. In other words, you may be expected to kill. Even worse, there is a reciprocal possibility that people will try to kill you. The reason no one expresses this clearly is that it's quite a bad deal.

No matter what the recruiter swears to you, there

is a very legal and serious hidden clause that says they have the right to ignore all their promises and put you to work wherever they need you – including combat.

So how do all these choices fail, thus justifying your going to Europe instead of attending college? Is this rational? How can it possibly work? Are you insane?

Think of this European expedition as your "walkabout." When a young Australian Aborigine approaches manhood, he sets off alone into the wilderness to prove he's ready to be an adult.

Likewise, the Mormon church sends its young men all around the world for two years as missionaries. This is meant to spread the word about their religion, but it's also a period of maturation for the young men, exposing them to the ways of the world and teaching them to manage their goals.

The Amish have *rumspringa,* a time when a young person is allowed to leave the familiar surroundings of the like-minded and be exposed to the rest of the world's peculiarities.

So college isn't the only path to knowledge. There are multitudes of unexpected paths to success and countless examples of successful people who never attended college.

If Herman Melville hadn't spent his twenties as a sailor on whaling ships, *Moby Dick* might have merely been a story about a white cow chasing someone around a pasture. Would he have been a

better writer if he'd gone to college? Really?

The father of our country, George Washington, never went to college. Although he traveled to Barbados at twenty-one (where he contracted smallpox), he received his "education" on his return when he commanded the Virginia militia during the French and Indian War, successfully leading a critical ambush in the initial battle. This experience led directly to his becoming Commander in Chief of the American Army and the first President of the United States. He didn't need a resume.

Benjamin Franklin traveled to London at an early age where he worked in a print shop instead of attending college. That experience helped him on his path to become a well known writer, as well as a renowned inventor and political figure. His time abroad, among other things, led to his becoming a diplomat to France during the Revolutionary War.

Even Jesus spent forty days in the wilderness. No college whatsoever.

Yes, of course, things have changed since those guys struck out on their own to make their fortunes, but talk to some adults in today's work force. Ask them what they studied in college. Many, many people do not work in their college field of study. In some cases it's because a different opportunity presented itself. Some of these people find that their interests have changed. Others are unable to find jobs that match their years of preparation. There are no guarantees.

This book offers that same guarantee – none whatsoever.

Nevertheless, you are going to take the money that you and your parents were planning to pay your college and you are going to spend it on yourself – in Europe. You are going to *invest* that money in yourself. And, along the way, you're going to have the time of your life.

Chapter Two

Travel the World? Really?

Amelia Earhart quit college on several occasions, never graduating, yet she was allowed to teach college. That may be all you need to know about college. (She was also interested in aviation.)

This is not about a gap year. If you can afford a gap year, that's great. Have fun.

This book is about all the kids who don't know what the hell they want to do and, for no good reason, are about to settle for some arbitrary college program and hundreds of thousands of dollars in student loan debt.

Colleges today push study abroad as a major asset of their programs. Granted, they want you to come to them first, and give them your money, but even they think you'd be better off somewhere else – *Europe.* They're subcontracting out their jobs and your education, frequently in conjunction with foreign schools of lesser reputations.

Independent study is also a big deal with colleges. It means a teacher only has to check in at intervals, leaving the student to sink or swim.

The central idea in this book is both an independent study and a study abroad. You're just cutting out the middle man.

As soon as you start thinking about college, you're asked repeatedly what you plan to major in. Maybe you're one of those people who knows. Perhaps you've always known. Those people exist.

Most kids, however, don't know what they want to do for the rest of their life. That's not too surprising when you think about all the choices available.

Some students approach college as a sort of buffet, where they will be exposed to many different things in many different classes, hopefully leading to something that excites them enough to pursue it – *for the rest of their lives.*

Unfortunately, many colleges are not set up for this. Yes, you'll be taking many different courses, but the choices are predetermined among a set number of required or prerequisite classes. Your choices of electives that you're actually curious about are quite limited.

Students who know their career interests are scooted along, while less certain students are encouraged to pick a major – any major – so they can fit in and get moving.

The truth is, you are not "supposed" to know what you want to do for the rest of your life at this age. Not yet.

How can the same parents that say you don't know enough to make choices in other matters of less import believe that you should make a career choice before you're ready?

Tell your parents to relax. Job recruiters say that the thing that stands out most on a resume is "study abroad."

Employers may glance at your college transcripts, but no one but your mother really cares what grade you made on any given math test or how you did on

some essay that you labored over for hours despite a terrible hangover. What they really want to know is what kind of person they might be hiring.

There's no real standardized way of analyzing things like creativity or life experience or how you get along with people, but a few things stand out as obvious. Employers want to hire people who have life experience and they know that anyone who has spent years traveling has been confronted by an endless number of difficult situations. Survival skills are always desirable, as are entrepreneurial skills.

Today's economy is global and people who speak multiple languages are in demand in businesses that deal internationally.

People who've spent four years nestled in the womb of some college don't know diddly.

You, however, will be able to say that you don't know *merde.*

Already you're way ahead of them.

People say that college isn't just about your studies, it's about networking – meeting friends that you'll stay in touch with for the rest of your life. Especially business friends.

Look around. Is that really likely? Wouldn't you rather be meeting people all over the world that are going places? Those people are already on their way.

You should join them.

Chapter Three

Why Europe?

Mick Jagger dropped out of the London School of Economics to sing with a childhood pal. As a result, today he can't adequately handle his own money and has to pay other people to do so.

This country was settled primarily by Europeans. As such, it's perfectly understandable for our forefathers to have looked back over their shoulder, both geographically and historically, for their education. Their European roots colored everything, from the Greek philosophers to Shakespeare to the French Revolution.

The remainder of the world was largely ignored,

and that hasn't changed much as far as general education is concerned. Asia, Africa, and South America are still unfairly marginalized. They build great civilizations, but nobody in the U.S. seems to care.

So, if our current education system is so Europe-centric, it would seem that the ideal place to study Europe would be – *Europe!*

That's where the early American settlers mostly came from. And, as a direct result of that, it's also where those forefathers looked as a pattern for their own educational system. They studied the classics, partly because that's all there was.

Not much has changed since then, so you'll be returning to the source of traditional learning and upon graduation will have the recycled equivalent of a Sixteenth Century education, plus a few updates.

It's the educational version of a game of "telephone" where things are repeated mindlessly until they become distorted and unrecognizable.

Things in Europe may be old, but they are the actual old things, not modern interpretations. The Coliseum is still there, although the lions are gone. The Tower of London still has its actual instruments of torture, ready and willing. The original weather-beaten gargoyles still spew water from Notre Dame Cathedral. The statue of David is the very statue of David that Michaelangelo handled personally. And so on.

Incidentally, while Europe is named in the title

of this book, the concept of going abroad applies equally to other continents and countries. Europe is the cliché, but this idea also works with China, Japan, Brazil, South Africa, India, and Israel, etc.

England, Scotland, and Ireland are certainly places of interest with rich histories, but that's cheating. Learning an accent or dialect isn't going to be helpful. Go somewhere with a language that challenges you. It may seem overwhelming at first, but if little kids can speak the language, how hard can it be?

You're going to find that Europeans hold a lot of differing views of our country. You're probably not going to change their minds, but you may come away with a better understanding of who we are.

On your journey abroad you'll be amazed by the many differences between us and them. We have the Emmys and Oscars. They have the Nobel Prize. We have Charmin. They have *bidets*. We have the Big Mac. They put mayonnaise on fries.

By the time you come home you're gonna know a lot of practical stuff. How to do laundry on the road. How to follow directions that you can't understand. You'll learn to haggle. You'll be able to drive on the wrong side of the road. You'll know all the metric terms instead of real units of measurement (but once you're back you'll never have to use them again).

Like the World War soldiers who brought home exotic sports cars and a taste for fine wines, you'll bring home your own imports to amaze and entertain your family and friends.

Even if you believe with all your heart that the U.S.A. is the greatest country of all, it won't hurt you to appreciate what the other countries are like and what they have to offer.

We like to think that we are able to be moral and benevolent because we are the mightiest country on Earth, and will be forever.

Thus, you'll enjoy visiting England, which itself once was the mightiest empire on Earth, indomitable and masters of the world far and wide, much like us. But not now.

You'll also notice when you visit Rome, which once ruled the majority of the known world, that things have changed there, too.

Spain was such an international powerhouse that to this day almost all of South and Central America still speak their language – as do Los Angeles and Texas.

Iran was called Persia when it was the most powerful nation on Earth, and they haven't given up, even if they've still got some work to do.

The Vikings conquered quite a few countries as they sought to dominate Europe. France was on its way to world conquest when Napoleon hit some bad weather in Russia. Everyone remembers Germany vying to take over the world in back to back attempts. Even the damned barbarians had a pretty good ride for a while, sweeping across Europe.

So things change. There might be a lesson there,

but who's to say?

You may be surprised to learn that a lot of Europeans do not want to emigrate to the U.S. They like their countries, eating weird food, and feeling that they are the center of the universe.

You may, too.

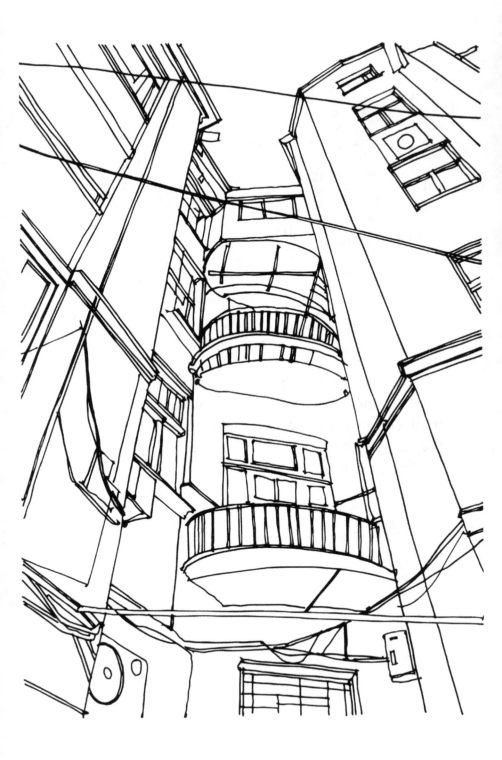

Chapter Four

Research?

Robert Fulton had an early education at a Pennsylvania Quaker school before abandoning it for the lure of London, where he hoped to become a painter. Fascinated with emerging technologies in Europe, he patented a machine for dredging canals and built a submarine called the Nautilus to enable Napoleon to attack the British. Upon returning to New York, he developed the first steamboat, revolutionizing travel by water.

Remember, this is not a vacation. You're not traveling to Europe, you're *moving* to Europe.

You won't be living at the Ritz for four years.

And, if you don't want to be camping in a hostel the whole time, you're going to need to find a place to *live* – not a place to stay.

Just the act of picking a country will require research. If you do well and find the best choice, you'll be rewarded with an excellent life. If you don't, you will suffer accordingly.

Do you speak a foreign language? Don't worry. You will. Or you'll starve.

Whatever country you choose, once you arrive you'll have to research the local area to find a place to live that (a) you can afford, and (b) will provide

access to learning. This requires a bit of study in geography, and perhaps a bit of sociology and economics. Enjoy.

It would be senseless to stay in one place the whole time. For instance, you might stay one year each in four different countries, say France, Italy, Germany, and Spain. This would give you an emphasis on different cultures and histories. Maybe you'll want to throw in something more obscure, like one of the Slavic or Scandinavian countries. It's all up to you.

Perhaps you'll follow several different interests, moving from one place to another. You could study Picasso in Spain and France, then move to Italy to learn about Leonardo da Vinci and Michaelangelo.

Or, marvel at the architecture in Barcelona, move to Germany to study Psychology, and then to Greece for the early classics or Archeology.

As a resident you won't be trying to see every-

thing in the Louvre in a single morning. Spend a week there if you like, or more. Consider an extended visit to Florence to study the art of the Medici. Take side trips to Morocco and Egypt. Check out the Kremlin.

Plan ahead for the good times, too. There's more to traveling in Europe than simply studying. There's Oktoberfest in Germany, Carnival in Venice, The Cannes Film Festival, any Formula One race, Tomorrowland Music Festival in Belgium, and Kings Day in the Netherlands. Eat crepes at the Maslenitsa Festival and then run with the bulls in Pamplona.

You can throw tomatoes at La Tomatina Festival in Buñol, Spain, or oranges at the Carnival of Ivrea, in Italy. Celebrate Bastille Day, San Gennaro Feast Day, St. Patricks' Day, and St. John's Day. It's your homework.

There will be no teachers telling you what you *must* study or what is inappropriate. Just because something is fun doesn't mean you won't learn from it.

Don't forget to send home plenty of postcards to needle your friends. Post selfies on Instagram from every great spot you visit. Post your favorite meals online as well. All in the name of research and study.

Communication is the first step in your job hunt, preparing the battlefield for when you return home. Send frequent reports to your parents because they'll spread the word. You'll become legend. And maybe they'll send money.

Facetime. Skype. Email. Text. Blog. Vlog. Instagram. Snapchat. Whatsapp. (Facebook is for amateurs. Avoid it.)

Chapter Five

Make a Plan

Charles Dickens quit school when his father went to debtor's prison. Subsequent life as a factory worker exposed him to the difficult social conditions that he would write about as he became one of the most popular novelists of his day.

Yes, you'll need a plan. It doesn't have to be a great plan or a complete plan. There will not be a teacher reviewing it or grading it. But – you're going to live it.

First, where do you want to go? Not sure? That's fine. What are you interested in? Is there a country or area that you've always been curious about? Is

31

there a family connection somewhere you'd like to investigate? A subject you've wondered about? A particular cuisine that beckons to you?

You can always change your mind, but what you need is a starting point. Your flight to Europe isn't going to circle endlessly until you make up your mind. It has to land somewhere and so do you. When you step out of the airport, where do you want to be?

Obviously the Internet is going to be your friend and advisor. It's filled with information about travel to Europe, however no one has checked it for accuracy. Some information is woefully out of date, while other things are outright lies and scams. Do your homework. Cross reference things.

What about language?

Google Translate is a great starting point and can help in an emergency, but you won't get a job because you know how to use it. Learning a language is critical, but it's not an insurmountable obstacle.

It's good to know that all pilots are required to speak English, so if a translation emergency arises, get to an airport and approach someone in a uniform for help.

There are many places that offer inexpensive immersive language opportunities and often they include living with a family that speaks that language. That gives you a place to stay and an introduction to life with the natives.

Chapter Six

Make a Budget

At 13, David Crockett ran away from school, pre-ferring life as a game hunter, a buckeroo on cattle drives, and farmer before rising to the rank of Lt. Colonel in the Tennessee militia. He entered county politics, was elected to the United States House of Representatives, and became a well known orator and public figure in the nation.

A *budget?* Don't be silly.

A budget presupposes an understanding of assets, expected expenses, and a somewhat predictable income that can all be balanced against one another.

You don't have any money. You don't know what

things are going to cost. You won't have an income.

Therefore, you don't need a budget. You need an *attitude*.

That attitude is (a) you can't afford it, and (b) you'll find a way.

It will seem like everything in Europe costs way too much money – and it does – so you're going to have to be frugal. Pick your expenditures carefully and make sure they're worth it. Then *enjoy!*

For instance, you may routinely be substituting a modest sandwich for any five-star dining experiences, but you can still nosh in spectacular settings, both in cities or the country. Enjoy lunching alongside the Thames or the Seine and enjoy the passing show. Dine at twilight in Paris as the lights come on all over the Eiffel Tower. Some European bars traditionally provide *tapas, hors d'oeuvres,* or munchies when you buy a drink. Chow down.

Buy or rent a bicycle instead of that Lamborghini you've always fantasized about. Or compromise on a Vespa. You'll learn about trains as you do the math to find out if the long term pass is cheaper than individual tickets. Like everything, it depends.

Lodging will always be an issue, unless you meet the love of your life who also has a little extra closet space. Search carefully and exhaustively for a modest place that is uncomfortable enough that you'll prefer being elsewhere. Maybe you'll need to share a place, so consider a roomie – you'd definitely have one if you were back home in college.

Everyone likes the word "free," but you're going to live for that word. You're going to *need* "free." That doesn't mean you're panhandling, but you're going to have to be creative.

Whether you're exploring Seville's *Plaza de España* or strolling through Belfast Castle for the

views of the city, there are free things to do. Watch the Glockenspiel perform the "Cooper's Dance" in Munich's Marienplatz or the changing of the guard at the Tomb of the Unknown Soldier in Warsaw.

Are these things educational? Damn straight.

The Internet provides multiple lists of free museums and galleries, but even the Louvre is free until you're 26. In fact, many prominent museums are free at different times. Plan ahead.

Just walking the historic streets of Europe is free. Parks are free, as are most sunsets. Music in the streets is free, whether it's a strolling gypsy or a string quartet in Venice's St. Mark's Square. There are free concerts. Libraries are free. Conversation everywhere is free. Play street chess in Salzburg for free. Visit great churches for free, including a view of Michaelangelo's "Madonna and Child" at

Onze-Lieve-Vrouwekerk. Even shopping is free, unless you buy something. Take advantage of all these things.

Be cheap, but don't forget that sometimes you have to splurge. If something is important to you, and you may not have another opportunity, spend the money. Create the memory. Get the selfie. Send it to someone who will eat their heart out.

Chapter Seven

Finances: The Bad News

Will Rogers left school at ten. At twenty he went to Argentina to be a gaucho, lost everything, and moved to South Africa, where he joined a circus headed for Australia. Vaudeville led to success after he roped a bull that charged the crowd. His broad life experience prepared him to become a popular performer, comedian, and newspaper writer.

College, as they say, isn't for everyone. And, it's priced accordingly.

A prestigious private college can easily exceed seventy thousand dollars a year. That's closing in on three hundred thousand dollars for a four-year edu-

cation. In addition, there can be substantial expenses for travel, meals, books, and incidentals. Many people take longer than four years to graduate.

The cheat is that not everyone pays that much. Some quite wisely choose a less expensive college. Some are granted scholarships and other benefits to reduce their costs. Many – far too many – resort to student loans for their tuition and living expenses. That's all fine, but other than the exception of a full ride or similar windfall, a college education is always more pricey than an airplane ticket to Europe.

The biggest challenge in this dubious endeavor is to convince your parents. You'll be old enough that you won't need their permission to travel abroad, but you're going to need their dough.

It's a tough sell to talk any adult out of large sums of money, but in this case you're also going against the conventional wisdom of "going to college."

Understandably, there are not many scholarships

for people who just want to go to Europe and the government certainly isn't going to give you a student loan for your trip. You're going to have to wheedle, promise, scheme, and lie, but you still won't be able to convince mom and dad. That's when you'll have to get creative. Make a deal. Any kind of deal. Whatever it takes.

For example, suppose your proposed college education is a "modest" thirty grand a year. Four years will still be over a hundred twenty thousand dollars that your folks will be on the hook for. You can be sure that they're already staring that obligation in the eye with great trepidation. Offer them a discount. Agree to settle for an even hundred thousand. Or whatever. Then have them provide that money to *you* – not a bunch of effete professors.

Your figures may vary, but this very negotiation is a life lesson that a conventional college education would never provide. Sensible parents are going to be resistant, but your perseverance will demonstrate commitment.

The prices that colleges charge for room and board are criminal. In reality, you're not going to eat that dining hall food anyway. You're certainly not going to be eating those dumb salads after the first week. You'll be grabbing burgers off-campus instead. You'll be chomping ramen. You'll have pizza delivered. Your meal plan will be abandoned and the school will keep your money.

If college were priced reasonably maybe it all

wouldn't be such a waste, but once student loans became easily available, the schools started raising their prices to kids with the full knowledge that the bills would all be covered out of desperation. Colleges quickly used this newfound funding to create more lush and desirable campuses that would attract even more students and their additional student loan tuition.

Student loans are really easy to get. So are the loans for a student's parents. These loans sit there while you go to school, accruing interest. They sit there after graduation for six months. No payments, just more interest. If you go to graduate school, the payments are delayed until you are done with school, except that the interest keeps building.

When you're finally done with all your schooling – and that day will come – the payments start, whether you can afford them or not. Even if you can't, the interest keeps going.

You can duck and dodge payments your whole life, but even when you're retired, the interest will still be going. When your Social Security kicks in, you may well find that there's nothing for you there. The student loan takes over and gets your retirement money until it's paid off. You and your diploma will be living on the street. Be careful.

While life in Europe is expensive, too, you're not going to be staying at five-star hotels, and maybe not even at one-star hotels. But you're not going to be camping either. You're going to learn to be creative. You'll be looking for affordable longer term housing. Maybe it will be a modest apartment, but it's probably just going to be a small room in someone's home. You won't be there much anyway.

You're going to make friends along the way, so maybe you'll find some wildly affordable (or free) arrangement to stay somewhere for an extended time. Sometimes you'll crash on someone's couch. It'll all work out.

You'll have to be thoughtful and careful about your expenditures abroad, but if worse comes to worst, you'll come home a little early with a higher, more compressed level of European experience.

Chapter Eight

The Good News

Thomas Edison spent his college age years developing entrepreneurial skills and learning about blue collar things such as electricity and wiring while working for Western Union. He applied that knowledge to a variety of inventions, becoming a captain of industry, but never received a diploma.

Perhaps the one thing worse than going to college is getting *into* college. Putting aside the fretting, the sweat, and all the unnecessary stress, plus the inevitable guilt for your multiple failures, the college application process is worse than flawed – it's insane.

Recent college entrance scandals have shined an

unpleasant light on the entire process as rich parents found secret, illegal ways to beat the system and get their kids into top schools.

The good news is that these self-important elitists have given all the other kids in the world an excuse for why they couldn't get into Stanford. "My space was taken by a rich kid."

One insipid parent paid six and a half million dollars to get a lucky, entitled child into college, evidently without realizing that if you can afford that, your child doesn't really need to go to college. Give the money to the kid instead, keep it in the family, or put it in a trust fund for the poor deprived child.

Better yet, take the money and send the kid to Europe for fifty years. That sum would provide $130,000 a year, plus interest, during that time. If a kid can't live on that, an education would just be a waste anyway.

You, however, don't have to worry about going to jail for bribing school officials or cheating on the SAT. Instead, you're going to skip over that entire admission process. You're already qualified to go to Europe.

There are no SAT or ACT exams required. No high-priced tutoring. No campus visits. No high pressure interviews. No tedious applications. No ridiculous essays. Best of all, no fees. *Bon voyage.*

Unless you're a convicted felon or a revolutionary, you'll be welcomed into any country in Europe. If you *are* a convicted felon or a revolutionary,

you'll have a reason to stay home and go to college – perhaps UC Berkeley.

On the other hand, if you decide to go to college instead of Europe, you'll have to go through the whole miserable admission process. Here's how it will go.

First, they'll make you take the PSAT, the *Preliminary* Scholastic Aptitude Test. You're obviously not going to be ready – that's why it's the preliminary version of the SAT – but, that's the test where they decide who gets the National Merit Scholarships. Apparently *those* kids were ready. You, however, are an unworthy screwup.

Those scores will give you something to worry about for a year or so, until you take the actual SAT or ACT exams. All this time your parents will be wondering if you need one of the many expensive tutorial programs available. All the other kids seem to be enrolling in them so they'll have an unfair advantage over you. They'll get your place in the college of your dreams! They'll also get all your scholarship money! You might as well just join the army now.

Either way, you'll take the SAT or ACT. Regardless of your scores – which are never good enough – you'll be on your way through the rest of the process. Your impersonal, totally objective test scores will be combined with a heartless evaluation of your essay portion of the SAT, followed by the hopelessness-inducing Achievement Tests.

The next phase, visiting colleges, is the worst. They all put on a show for potential recruits, making it look like college is mostly a lot of party events, with a few really fun classes thrown in for your parents' benefit. You'll take tours of modern classrooms, laboratories, dorms, and gymnasiums. Boring guides will cheerfully show off rooms filled with computers, as if that were somehow impressive today, even though no one needs big computers anymore.

There will be cafeterias that pretend to offer delicious food. You'll be given an opportunity to talk to current students who are paid to be outright shills. Maybe you'll visit an "actual" class being taught, all staged for the benefit of you and your parents.

You'll eventually narrow your school choices and start the application process. To make it easier on applicants, most of the colleges share the Com-

mon App. That is supposedly a labor-saving application that eliminates the need to repeatedly answer the same questions – except that most colleges then add their own special questions, totally negating the whole concept.

Next come the inane essays that you'll have to write on even more inane subjects. Your challenge is to stand out with your intellect, creativity, and prose, without seeming too far out of normal to blend in. That essay, depending on the school, may be evaluated alongside the essays of over a hundred thousand others applicants. That's a lot of competition for the average teenager. Good luck.

Instead of a written essay, some colleges will let you send in your own personal video glorifying your high school accomplishments. You'll want to avoid these schools, not because there's anything wrong

with them, but because the budding *auteurs* who get in there because of their movies will be insufferable.

Interviews, either in person or via the Internet, are a critical step in the process. You'll speak to someone at the college who will evaluate your readiness for higher education while assessing your "fit" for the individual school. These interviews are typically conducted by bored students who are just trying to complete the work obligation under their financial aid agreement. They don't care. They're just waiting for the lunch break.

Along the way, you'll probably need to apply for financial aid – scholarships, grants, work-study jobs, student loans, and parent loans. Every step in this process takes time, costs money, and induces stress.

After all this, you wait.

And wait.

And wait.

So, instead of fretting about rejection letters, imagine the expression on your high school counselor's face when you casually mention your plans to blow off college and travel to Europe for four years. He or she will be appalled. And envious.

Even the most jaded of your friends will think you're cool. You are.

Chapter Nine

Academics

Louis "Satchmo" Armstrong referred to his teen-age years playing trumpet on riverboats as "going to the University." It served him well, leading to a fifty year career as a world-famous musician and singer.

If you're not going to be enrolled in an actual school, what will you learn?

Perhaps the most obvious thing is a new **Language.** Language skills can be the discriminator in your coming job search. Whatever language you learn, it will give you a shot at all kinds of opportunities in the countries that speak it, as well as with

American businesses that deal with that country.

You're going to be moving around from one country to another. That means you'll be studying maps – **Geography** – and learning about other lands.

You won't be studying **Math,** but you'll be using it constantly. From the simplest forms, figuring out financial transactions between currencies of different countries, to more complex business decisions about pricing, travel, lodging, meals, and shopping, you'll be doing math.

You may abhor **Political Science** now, but once you're confronted with all the things going on around you in Europe, you'll absorb plenty. You may even find yourself in the occasional argument.

If you're not studying **Anthropology,** they're studying you. And your culture. And all your family.

You're also surrounded by social relationships and institutions so you've stumbled into **Sociology,** too.

Maybe you don't care about **Philosophy,** but you're going to encounter countless discussions about life and thinking that will eventually seem compelling and challenging.

The **Art** that will surround you in Europe is astounding. From the murals of Pompeii to the ceiling of the Sistine Chapel, you'll be able to see them close up – not in thumbnail photos in an **Art History** textbook. And there will be actual artists all around. You can discuss things with them or join them with your own artwork.

Photography is rampant. Point a camera anywhere and there's a shot. Digital photography is so cheap you can start your own museum.

Germany and Austria are teeming with **Psychology,** so watch what you say and do.

History? It's everywhere, so overwhelmingly a part of every moment, every place, that you can't avoid it. You might as well give up and absorb some of it. They've had a few wars "over there" that are worth studying. And a few kings and queens, with lots of palaces and peccadilloes. Ever seen a guillotine?

From opera to pop, **Music** is everywhere. Pick an instrument, or just listen. Compose something or follow the life stories of those who did. Many American jazz greats spent years in Paris, not college. It was good enough for Billie Holiday. Shouldn't you try, too? Even the Beatles played Germany endless-

ly when they were young in the hope that it would lead to something.

Dance reverberates across the continent, ranging from the most formal ballet to historic folk dances that are passed down from one generation to the next.

Architecture essentially grew up in Europe and it's still going strong. Some of the greatest buildings in history line the streets.

Wherever there's antiquity, **Archeology** will follow. Myths come to life and shadows tell stories.

They've been creating **Literature** since the beginning of time, so you can either study it or add to it with your own thoughts.

In the **Theatre,** they're still talking about that Shakespeare kid. Molière, too, plus a poet called Homer that predated "The Simpsons." Aristophanes was here, along with a guy named Sophocles. So catch one of the local shows while you're in the neighborhood.

And on and on....

But here's the trick. You're only going to study these things if you're interested. If not, you'll move on to something else until you're having fun.

If there's something that strikes your interest and you want more, there are optional courses everywhere. The original educational institutions that America copied long ago are still going strong. There are many night courses, too.

Maybe you'll want to stroll across the campus at Oxford or such. When you get back home you can comment casually, "When I was at the Sorbonne...."

Don't forget that there are online courses available everywhere, many of them originating right here in the U.S.A. You'll still be in touch.

Chapter Ten

What Will You Miss in College?

Before he was Alexander the Great, the Prince of Macedon had numerous teachers, ending with a particularly prominent tutor named Aristotle. Nevertheless, at 16, like many youths, Alexander had studied enough and quit school to join the army. In fact, he joined at the very top of the army, where he easily conquered most of the known world.

By skipping college you're going to miss a lot. Exams. Professors. Grades. Stress.

Also, if you don't go to college you won't be in a marching band. You won't have any laboratory courses. You won't be taking Physical Education classes. You won't have to survive on Ramen. You won't have seven o'clock classes. You won't have to dissect little animals.

More importantly, you won't have to compete for classes. You won't have to sit and listen to endless lectures in required courses *that you hate.*

There will be lots of beer in college. You might miss that, but try the wine in Alsace or Tuscany.

You'll miss some of the girls and boys, but there will be some of those overseas.

In many ways, today's college kids have a great time, excluding most of the food on campus. Student life can be quite rewarding, unless you're too busy doing important homework. Do you enjoy endless reading? How about writing essays with lots of footnotes and formal references? Dubious research?

College classes can indeed be illuminating. You'll see little pictures in books that show all the great art that is hanging in places like the Musée d'Orsay or the Rijksmuseum. You can also see photographs of magnificent buildings that line the avenues of Berlin and the boulevards of Madrid. There will be movies about fascinating things, like the excavations being done in the Greek Islands or the latest presentation of the Bolshoi ballet. It's almost like you're there in person – but you're not. You should be!

Professors love to exclaim about all the wonders that they saw in Europe when they were there and perhaps yours will, too. It'll be great, providing you get that one all-too-busy professor instead of his

struggling graduate student.

You won't go to football games and you won't be in a fraternity or sorority, but you can be your own valedictorian. That'll look pretty good on your resume.

Chapter Eleven

What If You're Dead Broke?

Mary Wollstonecraft Shelley's stepmother saw no reason to educate her, but she traveled extensively in Europe, spending time in the company of writers such as Coleridge, Wordsworth, Lord Byron, and husband Percy Shelley. At twenty-one, such a gathering led to her novel, Frankenstein.

Yeah, not everyone can afford this. It's not fair. With all due apologies, this idea is pretty much limited to people with money.

Not everyone's parents are able or willing to chip in on this great adventure. So what can you do? You'll have to get really creative. Life is full of challenges and this is a big one that you'll have to solve. That's the whole point of this exercise anyway.

Without funding you probably won't stay in Europe for four years, but do what you can. You certainly won't be staying in the best lodgings or eating the best food, but you won't starve either.

You're going to have to work harder and faster, but you can always find a way. You're young and full of potential. Show everyone.

Maybe you can find a way to borrow the money from a friend, relative, or mentor as an investment. Sell your car. Cash in your savings. Mortgage your yacht.

If all else fails, get a job and save your money until you can find a cheap off-season flight. Once you arrive, even if you're dead broke, you're an American and you're blessed. Take advantage of it.

Most countries won't allow you permission to work, so you won't be able to support yourself or make a living, but maybe you can make a little extra here and there under the table.

You're about to become an expert on life in Europe. Can you write reviews or articles that have value to someone? Can you create an Instagram account that people will follow? Are there other jobs you can do online? Perhaps building websites. Or providing photography. Maybe even some type of consulting if there's something you're good at. Perhaps you could do it online, connecting with some work back at home.

Can you play an instrument on the street? Can you pose as a struggling artist? Can you dance? Do you have friends coming to visit who could use an expert tour guide?

Have you noticed something that you miss from life in the U.S.A? Is there a way to import it?

Business is different from regular employment so if there's something you've discovered in Europe that doesn't yet exist in the American market, can you export it home? After all, someone thought to ship Perrier sparkling water all the way to America despite the absurd expense and regardless of the fact that it tastes bad. Who knew?

This kind of entrepreneurial experience is both invaluable to you and impressive to potential employers. It means you'll be learning about things such as shipping costs, currency exchange, taxes, import duties, transportation, and marketing.

The worst imaginable scheme to pay for your trip would be to accumulate a stack of credit cards and use those for your expenses. Then, when you returned home steeped in debt, you'd probably have to declare bankruptcy and dismiss all your debt. (In contrast, student loans cannot be dismissed in a bankruptcy.)

Chapter Twelve

Plan B

Phineas Taylor Barnum left school at fifteen when his father died, forcing him into many jobs to support his family. A natural showman, he became a wildly successful promoter of freaks and oddities. With partner James Bailey he developed their circus into the Greatest Show on Earth.

There are always alternatives – last resorts.

If there's no way you can raise the money, but are determined enough, there's still hope because it's possible you can find some financial aid in more unusual ways, such as internships or volunteering.

They are not a free ride, and you'll be giving up

69

some of your free time, but they can be an important and helpful part of your financial aid package.

One of the big scams for colleges is their ability to get you an internship. This is good for them because they build relationships with local businesses by providing free student labor and they don't have to pay teachers to teach. And, they still collect your tuition, rent, and food expenses.

Internships typically offer you a chance to work in exchange for some sort of experience or training. They may be paid or unpaid, and there may be expenses for travel, etc. Not surprisingly, unpaid internships are usually easier to get.

You may not be able to work for hire in foreign countries, but you can usually work in an "internship" for free (check local regulations to make sure). An internship will gain you local experience in the field of your choice, but the more important advantage is that you build relationships that way. It's hard for anyone to resist free help, particularly if the helper is knowledgeable and industrious.

Granted, you may encounter relationships that are abusive, wasteful, or worse, but you can just quit. Find something else. It's a big world.

Volunteering is just work. It may be good work that is totally worthwhile and rewarding, but it may also be grueling work and offer only meager living conditions.

Specify FREE when you search for internships or volunteer opportunities. Check them out thor-

oughly. Research. Research. Research. And, oddly enough, you need to understand that free is not free.

When you search for Free internship or volunteering opportunities, usually the first thing you'll get are explanations of why "free" costs money. There can be hidden expenses – exchange rates, insurance costs, foreign transaction fees, medical expenses and costs for wifi, hot water, and linens. Don't be surprised to learn that you have to provide your own transportation.

Experiences in this arena vary and there are many

stories about the pitfalls of volunteering. Fortunately there are exceptions, but you'll have to dig deep, and once you find them, make sure they're not overselling, or worse yet – scams. You don't want to get trapped in some obscure place where you can't afford to get home.

One volunteering example, Worldwide Opportunities on Organic Farms (WWOLF), offers connections in many countries. You provide your own transportation and some other expenses, but you will work alongside farmers in other countries on organic farms. You are not paid for this work because it is an educational and cultural opportunity. Just like college.

Another possibility, the Peace Corps, typically requires a college degree – which somewhat invalidates the premise of this book. However, there are some exceptions if you have five years in a particular field. Maybe you've worked on a farm. Maybe you're a computer guru. Maybe you have another special skill that is needed somewhere. There is an additional program called Peace Corps Response that requires shorter time commitments, but requires professional experience or previous Peace Corps experience. One advantage of the Peace Corps is that some travel expenses are paid. Some volunteers get paid. Not many. Probably not you. But check.

You already speak a foreign language. It's not foreign in the U.S., but it's pretty foreign abroad. Believe it or not, you're qualified to teach it. You just have to find people who know less than you do – and there are plenty of those people overseas. You can teach English as a second language all over the world, except for a few places like England, Australia, and maybe Canada (arguable).

Plus, when you teach abroad you may have the chance to apply for a TEFL, TESL, or other certificate at the end of your program. Some programs offer classes leading to certification.

Diverbo offers a week in Spain or Germany where you spend time speaking English to people anxious to practice their language skills. You pay transportation costs to get there, but most other expenses are covered. There is a branch of this company designed especially for teenagers.

Some countries have programs of "repatriation" and sponsor visits by people who are descendants of that country. Hungary, Greece, Armenia, and Israel offer such programs. Some include transportation.

Another inventive way to spend time in some

countries is house sitting. It can be short term or long term. Usually the house-sitter pays all transportation costs and, in certain long term situations, may pay some of the home's expenses (such as utilities). A house-sitter may be responsible for some ongoing upkeep and maintenance matters as well, perhaps doing gardening chores or shoveling show. Pet sitting may or may not be part of the arrangement.

There are travel/tour companies that offer interesting opportunities. If you can organize eleven people to go on a tour together, the twelfth travels free. That's you. That's going to be a lot of work, but it's free.

Europe is filled with schools that host study abroad courses for U.S. colleges, but typically these courses are linked to an established college or university. That makes sense of course, but there are some internships that are available to non-students. You'll have to dig hard to find them, but they exist. There may be costs and fees associated with these internships, so do your research.

If you specialize in certain sports, such as skiing, snowboarding, windsurfing, or sailing, there are jobs available in many countries that provide pay and also assist with accommodations and meals. Some of these jobs have long term possibilities.

Believe it or not, crowdfunding is a possible way to get some financing for your journey – especially if you're volunteering for a worthwhile cause. It's worth a try.

As the ultimate last resort there's the French Foreign Legion, but it requires a five year commitment and living conditions can be marginal. Not recommended.

Chapter Thirteen

Love on the Run

Michelangelo di Lodovico Buonarroti Simoni had no interest in school, preferring to waste his time hanging out with artists and copying frescoes in local churches. At 13 he became an apprentice, but soon turned his attention to sculpture. His interest in religious artwork led to numerous frescos and sculptures of note.

A traditional part of the college fantasy is the notion that you may find the sweetheart of your dreams, fall in love, and start a lifetime of sharing and bliss.

Yeah, maybe. That happens.

Before you get too caught up in that particular fantasy, ask yourself if you really want to marry someone who can't get into a better college than you did. Be honest.

Putting marriage aside, college is a fetid swampland of romantic possibilities. There will be a swarm of alluring people who are, generally speaking, at your same level of hormonal disarray. There will be dances and concerts and football games and flirting and drinking and on and on. Along the way you'll have study groups and lab partners and shared bathrooms and rivals galore. Is that what you had in mind? If so, go for it. Jump into the seventy thousand dollar a year dating pool.

Naturally, at some point in any college curriculum you'll study some of the great romances of history, music, art, and literature. And not just Romeo and Juliet – as if that wasn't bad enough. Did you hear that Agamemnon loves Clytemnestra? You can learn the heartbreaking lessons of Tristan and Isolde. There's the oft-told tale of Caesar and Cleopatra. And then Mark Anthony pops up with that same Cleopatra. Remember Napoleon and Josephine? Consider Arthur and Guinevere, then Lancelot and Guinevere. Oedipus and Jocasta. Isabella of Castile and Ferdinand of Aragon. Vladimir Lenin and Inessa Armand. Good ol' Menelaus and Helen – then Paris and Helen. Eloise and Abelard. Dante and Beatrice. Cyrano and Roxanne. Don Quixote and Dulcinea. And on and on down through the centuries.

You'll notice that many of these love stories didn't work out (they'd all be dead by now anyway), but don't give up on true love. Not surprisingly, none of the world's great romances are about frat boys or cheerleaders or collegiate lovers of any stripe. They're all *European*.

So, let it be known that Europe is wide open territory for lovers and would-be lovers. And face it

– college would be full of the same types of people you weren't so crazy about in high school, just a few years older. Maybe the zits will be gone, but the personalities are still typical and predictable – because everyone is pretty much the same.

Maybe you're wondering – are you worthy of European affection? You're merely a high school graduate exploring some of the greatest civilizations on earth.

Why not? When you get to Europe, you'll be considered exotic. You'll be a good target for potential lovers – and not just people looking for a green card.

Close your eyes and imagine the difference between "dating" and "romance." Are you looking for a frat boy, a beauty queen, a cowboy, a prospective doctor, a cheerleader, a promising attorney, or even a potential President of the United States? If you are, that's fine. They'll probably still be single when you return from Europe.

Or – would you rather find someone who comes from royalty? Maybe you'd fancy an opera star or a ballerina. How about a revolutionary? A vintner. A fashionista. A diplomat. A poet. An expatriate. A Cordon Bleu chef. A matador. A smuggler. A Swiss banker. A Romanian fashion model. A French Legionnaire. A spy. Take your choice, or try them all.

Going to Europe is not exactly joining a monastery or convent. You will find temptations aplenty and you'll be swapping smiles in no time, trying to conquer new languages on the run. There is no European nationality going extinct for lack of lovemaking and those post-lunch *siestas* are not just about taking a nap. Cultures may vary greatly, but underneath it all, everybody sweats. By the time you come home, you'll be a wily veteran on matters of the heart. It will be quite educational.

Chapter Fourteen

Play Hard

*The closest an "incorrigible" young George Her-
man Ruth Jr. got to college was attending a refor-
matory, St. Mary's Industrial School for Boys, but
the time he spent hitting baseballs on the streets of
Baltimore would produce a legendary career as the
preeminent slugger of his day.*

If you'd received a college athletic scholarship
you wouldn't be reading this book, so you're probably more of a fan than a jock. Certainly college
offers lots of opportunities to attend exciting sports
events, but you can also find that same excitement
in Europe while also learning about new games.

You won't be watching college football, except possibly online, but you might find the occasional NFL game in certain cities. You may fear that you'll have to substitute futbol for football, but not necessarily. There is something called "Medieval football" which refers to a range of games, dating back to the Middle Ages, that were invented and played in various parts of Europe. They're called things like folk football, mob football, and Shrovetide football – and they're pretty rough.

If that doesn't work for you, there are other games available. Maybe you've heard of the Olympics. Europe is where they started and they're still going strong, but there are lots of other choices. If you look hard, you can find NBA games of a sort and the odd baseball or softball league. If you want spectacle, check out the horse racing or auto racing. The ponies run at swank events such as the famous *Prix de l'Arc de Triomphe* at Longchamp Racecourse. Formula One offers unbeatable color, drama, and excitement at glamorous auto races like the Monaco Grand Prix If you're looking to participate in sports, not just spectate, there are many standard sports that you'll be familiar with: tennis, boxing, ice hockey, rowing, volleyball, golf, cycling, sailing, etc. And there are quite a variety of games that are generally less well known to Americans: cricket, squash, rugby, falconry, fencing, mountaineering, pigeon racing, curling, jousting, and bullfighting.

If you want something even more obscure, consider taking up pétanque, shinty, bando, gurning, shinny, tossing the caber, or black pudding throwing.

If you prefer your games in a pub or a saloon, you'll be able to find things like snooker and darts.

If none of these appeal to you, bring a frisbee.

Chapter Fifteen

Trouble

Leon Trotsky abandoned his promising math studies to explore other interests and spent too much of his youth in a Russian prison instead of college. He traveled to various prisons, notably Nikolayev, Kherson, Odessa, and Moscow, until he was exiled to Siberia where he quietly studied philosophy. After escaping in a hay wagon, he became an influential writer in England.

Just like you can get kicked out of college, you can get kicked out of Europe – although it makes a much better story.

There are definitely things you can't do in other

lands. Drugs. Crimes. Don't start any revolutions.

There are neighborhoods in every city that you should stay out of. Europe is no different. Don't get crazy.

Be careful crossing borders. Be respectful of the police. Don't expect to have all the same rights and privileges that you have at home.

You're going to be meeting a lot of people and, just like at home, they're not all nice. Be prudent in your conversations and don't be too overeager to make friends. You don't want to be in the next sequel to "Taken," with Liam Neeson trying to track you down.

You've probably heard stories about pickpockets. They're not just in cute foreign films. They're real and they hang out in places frequented by tourists. Be careful and be smart.

Write down the phone number of the U.S. Embassy. Not in your cell phone or wallet – that's going to be stolen first.

Plan ahead for emergency situations. Know where the closest hospital is and understand the health insurance rules of the country you're visiting.

Don't forget to check out the State Department website for health and safety information on the area you're traveling to.

Watch your mouth. You may not speak their language, but they can probably understand yours.

2781

Chapter Sixteen

When You Come Home, Then What?

Like most jazz musicians of his time, trumpeter Miles Davis was a dropout. In his early twenties he was said to claim that his first visit to Paris "changed the way I looked at things forever."

The only "test" in the whole process is this. Will you be able to get a job? *Oui! Da! Si! Ja!*

Everybody gets a job. Your goal is to get a better job because of your experience abroad. You won't have any grades or a diploma, but it won't matter.

What would you think if you heard someone say, "I've been living in Europe for four years."

Most people would quickly think of the idle

rich, but also would imagine that this person must be successful. Either of those things is good in this context. This kid is obviously experienced in international travel, customs, and cultures.

Here are some tips for your job search.

Create a resume as you go. Make notes of anything you studied along the way and any special interests you've developed.

Emphasize your language skills, even partial fluency.

If you had an "internship," mention it. Exaggerate, but be smart about it.

Keep your addresses abroad, both an actual mail address and an email address. It keeps you international.

You probably know enough to become an inter-

national "consultant" about *something*. Start a business, even if it's something simple (with an impressive title).

Don't forget to make up some business cards and official stationery. If you can, build a website.

Use a bilingual greeting on your phone message.

Grades? Who cares about grades? You're going to have incredible letters of recommendation (even if you have to write them yourself).

It's probably pretty rare for someone to call a reference in Europe, especially if they don't speak the same language.

And another thing. When you get back, you won't be getting polite letters from your college for the rest of your life asking you to make a donation toward the education of others. You're welcome.

While your high school pals are paying off their student loans, you'll be returning to visit your friends in Europe. If you've kept your business going, you'll be able to write it all off as a business trip. If not, we'll call it post-graduate study.

A Letter to Your Poor Parents.

To Whom It May Concern:

I'm sorry. Really.

This all started out as a silly joke, but somehow it started to make sense. Now all your dreams for your child have been shattered. Oh well.

I hope for your sake that any of your additional children will not read this book.

The good news is – instead of traveling to sit in a boring, uncomfortable graduation ceremony where some distant caped figure walks across a stage to get a diploma he or she will never read – you can visit your child *in Europe.*

You'll be amazed at what this kid knows now, including multilingual slang, handy shortcuts, and cooking secrets. You'll have your own personal international tour guide, eager to impress. The aforementioned youth will have new friends, a faster gait, and a new outlook.

If he or she decides to return to the U.S., and has enough money left for an airline ticket, he or she will welcome life there anew, fully enriched for a successful life and job search.

Regards,
Anonymous

FINAL EXAM

This test is to justify the true academic nature of your time in Europe.

1. How many times did you fall in love?
   a. Gazillion
   b. All of the above.

2. How much did you spend on textbooks?_____

3. Did anyone ask how you did on the SAT? _____

4. Did you marry someone who needs a Green Card?
Yes.___ No.____ Not sure.____

5. Did you miss your wonderful parents?
Of course.___Every moment.___ Who?___

6. What was your favorite meal? _____

7. What was your favorite dessert? _____

8. How many languages did you encounter? _____

9. Did you learn to speak with an accent? _____

10. Did it work with him/her? Yes.____ No.____

11. How many times did you smile? _____

12. Did you get lost? Yes.___ No.___ Always.___

13. Did you engage in espionage? _____

_____

14. Gnocchi or escargot? (Circle one)

15. Oktoberfest or Halloween? (Circle one)

16. Cubism or Nazism? Contrast and compare.

_____

_____

17. Write something impressive here._____

_____

_____

18. How was the weather? _____

19. What was your favorite cheese? _____

20. Why did you come back? _____

_____

_____

Grade it yourself on the honor system. Pick a grade.
Any grade. No one is going to care.

If you survived four years in Europe, you are entitled to receive this distinguished document.

European Vacation/College-Equivalency Diploma.

Be it known to all that

INSERT NAME HERE

has met all requirements of European travel and is entitled to henceforth be known as a Graduate of International Travel to Europe.

With Distinction

Now go find a job.

The Don't-Go-to-College
Money-back Guarantee

We fully warrant that if you buy this book, dutifully and faithfully apply the actions outlined therein, spend a full four years abroad, yet fail to find the experience educational, we will give you all your money back (exclusive of shipping, packaging, postage, and any and all taxes) pertaining specifically and exclusively to the money you spent on this book (retail price only) – not the trip to Europe.

This will be paid upon presentation of the original receipt for the book and an accounting of your four years of expenses, accompanied by all receipts, duly notarized.

About the Author

Jimmy Huston grew up on college campuses where his father was first a graduate student, then later a college professor. He occasionally attended college himself, somehow managing to graduate, and has forced two daughters to attend college. He has even taught college. And, he believes that college is a crock.

www.byjimmyhuston.com
jh@byjimmyhuston.com

Reviews are usually appreciated.

Other Odd Books by Jimmy Huston

Dead Is the New Sick: An Insider's Guide to Senility, Paranoia, and Curmudgery.

The I Hate to Read Book

The Dyslexic Hanbdook: Genius Edition!

Cussing for Kids: Etiquette for the Profane

Nate-Nate the Christmas Snake.

How to Write This Book

Is This Your First Funeral?

Why Can't Mommy Spend More Time with Me?

All are available at *www.cosworthpublishing.com* and on Amazon.

CPSIA information can be obtained
at www.ICGtesting.com
Printed in the USA
FFHW020210160519
52484917-57916FF